D0518902

ARIEL BOOKS

**Andrews McMeel
Publishing**

Kansas City

Grandmother

Grandmother

For information write Andrews McMeel
Publishing, an Andrews McMeel Universal company,
4520 Main Street, Kansas City, Missouri 64111.

Design & artwork by Junie Lee Tait
Edited by Sue Carnahan

ISBN: 0-7407-1952-1
Library of Congress Catalog Card Number: 2001086641

Grandmother

Loveliest of women!

Heav'n is in thy soul,

Beauty and virtue shine

for ever round thee.

—JOSEPH ADDISON

We have become a grandmother.

—*Margaret Thatcher*

A thousand Dreams

BURN SOFTLY INSIDE ME . . .

—Arthur Rimbaud

MY HEAD IS COVERED WITH

a glorious turban

OF GREY.

—Meshullam da Piera

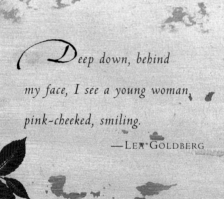

Deep down, behind

my face, I see a young woman,

pink-cheeked, smiling.

—LEA GOLDBERG

. . . *t*ough,

self-renewing,

AN ENDURING WEALTH,

passing through generations . . .

—*Sophocles*

She had kingly power

O'er the young soul.

— Lydia Howard Sigourney

Family faces . . .

magic mirrors.

— GAIL LUMET BUCKLEY

THEOPHILIS, DAUGHTER
OF CLEOCHA, MADE IT—

DAUGHTER, MOTHER,

GRANDMOTHER

woven in the thread.

—*Nossis*

BONE OF MY BONE,

AND *flesh* OF MY *flesh*.

—GENESIS 2:23

Ah! how great the world is by lamplight!

How small the world is in the eyes of memory!

—*Charles Baudelaire*

I love my past.

I love my present.

I'M NOT ASHAMED OF WHAT I HAD,

AND I'M NOT SAD BECAUSE

I HAVE IT NO LONGER.

—Colette

L o o κ, how they scold me

for all my L O V I N G and tippling,

now that the S I L V E R Y edges

S H I N E forth from my brow!

—*Abu Yahya*

$\mathcal{E}$ven now

I AM NOT OLD.

I never think of it, and yet

I AM A GRANDMOTHER

to eleven grandchildren.

—Grandma Moses

MEMORY IS A NET:

ONE FINDS IT FULL OF FISH

WHEN HE TAKES IT

FROM THE BROOK,

BUT A DOZEN MILES OF

WATER HAVE RUN THROUGH

IT WITHOUT STICKING.

—*Oliver Wendell Holmes Sr.*

What feeling is so nice as

a child's hand in yours? So

small, so soft and warm, like

a kitten huddling in the

shelter of your clasp.

—Marjorie Holmes

I'm still a child.

—*Amir Gilboa*

DRIVEN ON CEASELESSLY
TOWARDS NEW SHORES . . . SHALL WE
NEVER CAST ANCHOR FOR

A SINGLE DAY IN THE

OCEAN OF TIME?

—*Alphonse de Lamartine*

Menu
EUROPÉEN

I AM THE FAMILY FACE;

FLESH PERISHES,

I LIVE ON,

PROJECTING TRAIT

AND TRACE . . .

—*Thomas Hardy*

YOUR DESCENDANTS

shall gather your fruits.

Virgil

As you are at *seven*,

so you are at *seventy*.

—*Jewish proverb*

ONLY HER MIRROR REMAINED IN THE HOUSE. . . .

And I, her pale

granddaughter,

who do not

resemble her,

look into it today as

if into a lake that

HIDES ITS TREASURES BENEATH THE WATER.

—LEA GOLDBERG

AT THE DECLINE OF DAY

WE RECALL BOTH

THE FRESH MORNING

AND THE BRILLIANCE

AND HEAT OF NOON.
—*Prince Pëtr Vyázemsky*

WHATEVER IT IS—

SHE HAS TRIED IT—

— *Emily Dickinson*

She teaches the girls,

And she warns the boys . . .

And increases their gain

By her orderly reign.

—FRIEDRICH VON SCHILLER

*I*F YOU HAVE KNOWLEDGE,

LET OTHERS LIGHT

THEIR CANDLES IN IT.

—*Margaret Fuller*

Children require

GUIDANCE AND SYMPATHY

far more than instruction.

—Anne Sullivan

STORYTELLING . . .

THE OLDEST FORM

OF EDUCATION.

—*Terry Tempest Williams*

Grandma told me all about it,

Told me so I couldn't doubt it,

How she danced, my grandma danced; long ago . . . .

—MARY MAPES DODGE

NEW SHOOTS,

EVERY YEAR;

ON OLD GROWTHS APPEAR . . .

—*Lucy Larcom*

*I*t's not for this

I color my hair

black—

to look younger

and learn more

wildness . . .

—*Rudagi*

The jelly—the jam

and the marmalade,

And the cherry and quince

"preserves" she made!

—*James Whitcomb Riley*

We are

too soon

old and too

late wise.

—JEWISH PROVERB

*. . . W*ith affections warm,

intense, refined,

She mixed such calm and

holy strength of mind . . .

—Thomas Campbell

Anxiously fond,
though oft her spectacles
With elfin cunning hid,
and oft the pins
Drawn from her ravelled stocking,
might have soured
One less indulgent.
—Anna Laetitia Barbauld

They pampered me,

especially my grandmother. .

I loved her with all my heart.

—CAMARA LAYE

All the way back

to my youth

my heart travels . . .

—Abu Nasr of Gilan

A shadow in the

parching sun,

and a shelter in

a blustering storme.

—Anne Bradstreet

... *One never* R E G R E T S

... *one's* M I S T A K E S.

— *Oscar Wilde*

When the voices of children

are heard on the green

And whisp'rings are in the dale;

The days of my youth rise fresh in my mind . . .

— William Blake

It's not

as it was

when I was young.

—LIU YUNG

Hours, you are briefer than kisses
        the sun's lips leave on the mournful sea,
briefer than cries of migrating birds
        dropping their pearls of song,
briefer than brilliant glints from the shell
        a scurrying beetle wears as a shield,
briefer than hands parting in farewell . . .

—ANNETTE VON DROSTE-HÜLSHOFF

grandma

THE DAYS MAY COME, THE DAYS

MAY GO,

BUT STILL THE HANDS OF MEMORY

WEAVE.

—*George Cooper*

How unspeakably the

lengthening of memories

in common endears our

old friends!

— *George Eliot*

WHERE I WAS BORN

THE FLOWERS HAVE ALWAYS

THE SAME SCENT . . .

—KI NO TSURAYUKI

O TIME, SUSPEND YOUR FLIGHT! AND YOU, FORTUNATE HOURS, STAY YOUR JOURNEY! LET US SAVOUR THE FLEETING DELIGHTS OF THE FINEST OF OUR DAYS!

—ALPHONSE DE LAMARTINE

Life engenders life.

Energy creates

energy. It is by

spending oneself

that one becomes

rich.

—Sarah Bernhardt

If a child is to keep alive

his inborn sense of wonder . . .

he needs the companionship of

at least one adult who can share it,

rediscovering with him the joy,

excitement, and mystery

of the world we live in.

—RACHEL CARSON

$\mathcal{L}$ooking at people who belong to us,

we see the past, present, and future.

—GAIL LUMET BUCKLEY

...*to* be the

candle or the

mirror that

reflects it.

— *Edith Wharton*

... She is the teeming

MOTHER OF MOTHERS

... the bearer of them

that shall grow and

...E MATES TO THE MOTHERS.

—WALT WHITMAN

WHEN YOU HAVE A GRANDCHILD,

YOU HAVE TWO CHILDREN.

—JEWISH PROVERB

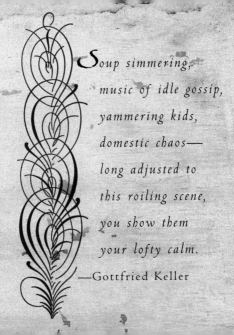

Soup simmering,
music of idle gossip,
yammering kids,
domestic chaos—
long adjusted to
this roiling scene,
you show them
your lofty calm.

—Gottfried Keller

*Y*ou are BEAUTIFUL . . .

Like an old opera tune

Played upon a harpsichord.

—*Amy Lowell*

She was like the S U N ,

        making red, in her R I S I N G ,

The clouds of dawn with the flame of her light.

                         —Judah ha-Levi

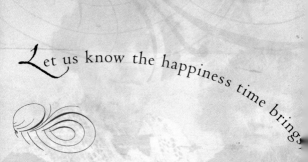

Let us know the happiness time brings.

not count the years.

—Ausonius

She sits, looking at the sun
going down, and weaves and talks
with the neighbors, and thinks back
to when she dressed up
fine for holidays
and danced all night—
so lithe, so firm—with the boys,
her escorts through
that season of light.

—GIACOMO LEOPARDI

*Y*OU ARE THE BOWS

FROM WHICH YOUR CHILDREN

AS LIVING ARROWS

ARE SENT FORTH.

—*Kahlil Gibran*

. . . *So wise and right and*

tender a heart, that it

was as good as genius.

— MARGARET OLIPHANT

As is the generation of leaves,

so is that of humanity.

The wind scatters the leaves

on the ground,

but the live timber burgeons

with leaves again in

the season of spring . . .

—*Homer*

Our mothers and grandmothers . . .

moving to music not yet written.

—*Alice Walker*

A grandam's name
is little less in love
than is the doting
title of a mother.

—*William Shakespeare*

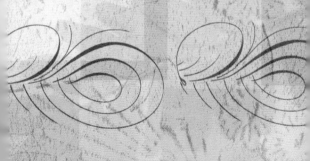

She is a tree of life to them.

— *Proverbs 3:18*

When she left she always kept

the door slightly unlatched. . . .

She always called in a whisper,

"Good night my sweet sparrows."

—LORRIE MOORE

One life of so much consequence!

Yet I—for it—would pay—

My soul's *entire income*—

In ceaseless—salary—

—EMILY DICKINSON

$\mathcal{L}$et us L O V E then,

let us L O V E ! be quick to

enjoy the fleeting hour!

—Alphonse de Lamartine

No Spring nor Summer Beauty

hath such grace

As I have seen in one

Autumnal face.

—John Donne

'TIS A HIGH VIRTUE
TO TREAD IN THE
STEPS OF OUR
ANCESTORS, WHEN
THEY HAVE GONE
BEFORE US IN THE
RIGHT PATH.
—*Pliny the Younger*

So unaffected, so composed, a mind,

So firm, yet soft, so strong, yet so refin'd.

—Alexander Pope

You are the sun, grandma,

you are the sun in my life.

—Kitty Tsui

To forget one's ANCESTORS

is to be a brook without a SOURCE,

a tree without ROOT.

—*Chinese proverb*

Those shadowy recollections . . .

Are yet the fountain-light of all our day,

Are yet a master-light of all our seeing . . .

—William Wordsworth

...*and* they said, "YOU ARE SILVER!"

My answer: "WHAT OF IT?

If the sun lights up my hair,

IS THIS NOT CAUSE FOR JOY?"

—Ibn Ghaiyath

O Heart's memory,
    you are stronger than the mournful
memory of reason;
        and often in a distant land
you bewitch me with your sweetness.

—*Konstantin Bátyushkov*

Thou wert my guide, philosopher, and friend.

— Alexander Pope

*N*ow that I've reached the age . . .
where I need my children more
than they need me,
I really understand
how grand it is to be a grandmother.

—Mrs. Margaret Whitlam

I shall feel no regret for roses which have faded with the passing of fleeting spring; I also love the grapes on the vine, which have ripened in bunches beneath the hill.

—Aleksándr Púshkin

$\mathcal{S}$o many

things we

love are

you!

— *Anne Morrow Lindbergh*

I DRINK IN LONG DRAUGHTS

THE WINE OF MEMORY . . .

—CHARLES BAUDELAIRE

I console old people

when they grieve;

Loving fun,

to the young

I am a friend.

—Songs of Milarepa

Rappelle-toi . . .

Remember . . .

—*Alfred de Musset*

No moon,

it is not spring,

and only I

am the same.

—ARIWARA NO NARIHIRA

Though I look old,

yet I am

STRONG AND LUSTY . . .

—*William Shakespeare*

. . . teach me your gift of good life;

if your advice is sound,

I'll praise you forever . . .

—HUW LLWYD

*T*HERE ARE GRAY HAIRS

IN MY HEAD;

THERE IS FROST

ON THE MEADOWS,

BUT I GO ON DREAMING . . .

OF LIFE'S ENDLESS SPRING . . .

—*Rosalía de Castro*

$\mathcal{F}$LOW, FLOW, FLOW,

the current of life is ever onward.

—*Kobo Daishi*

Notes

Abu Nasr of Gilan (10th century), "A Memory of Youth"

Abu Yahya (13th century), "Late Flowering"

Addison, Joseph (1672–1719), *Cato*, 1713

Ariwara No Narihira (9th century)

Ausonius (c. 310–395)

Barbauld, Anna Laetitia (1743–1825), "Washing-Day"

Bátyushkov, Konstantín (1787–1855), "My Spirit"

Baudelaire, Charles (1821–1867), *La Chevelure* (p. 98); *Le Voyage* (p. 17)

Bernhardt, Sarah (1844–1923)

Blake, William (1757–1827), "Nurse's Song"

Bradstreet, Anne (1612–1672)

Buckley, Gail Lumet (1937–)

Campbell, Thomas (1777–1844), *Theodric*

Carson, Rachel (1907–1964), *The Sense of Wonder*

Castro, Rosalía de (1837–1885)

Colette (1873–1954), *The Last of Cheri*, 1926

Cooper, George (1838–1927), "Sweet Genevieve," 1877

Dickinson, Emily (1830–1886), "248" (p. 81); "1200" (p. 35)

Dodge, Mary Mapes (1838–1905), "The Minuet," *Along the Way*, 1879

Donne, John (1572–1631), "To Lady Magdalen Herbert"

Droste-Hülshoff, Annette von (1797–1848), "In the Grasses"

Eliot, George (1819–1880)

Fuller, Margaret (1810–1850)

Gibran, Kahlil (1883–1931), "On Children," *The Prophet*, 1923

Gilboa, Amir (dates unknown), "Moses"

Goldberg, Lea (dates unknown), "From My Mother's House"

ha-Levi, Judah (1075–1141)

Hardy, Thomas (1840–1928), "Heredity," *Moments of Vision*, 1917

Holmes, Marjorie (1910–), *Calendar of Love and Inspiration*, 1981

Holmes, Oliver Wendell, Sr. (1809–1894)

Homer (c. 9th century), *The Iliad*

Huw Llwyd (c. 1568–c. 1630), *"Cyngor y Llwynog"*

Ibn Ghaiyath (1141–1222), "White Hair"

Keller, Gottfried (1819–1890), "Venus de Milo"

Ki No Tsurayuki (882–946)

Kobo Daishi (774–835)

Lamartine, Alphonse de (1790–1869), *Le Lac*

Larcom, Lucy (c. 1826–1893), "Plant a Tree"

Laye, Camara, *The Dark Child*, 1954

Leopardi, Giacomo (1798–1837), "Saturday Night in the Village"

Lindbergh, Anne Morrow (1906–)

Liu Yung (dates unknown), "Tune: Wanderings of a Youth"

Lowell, Amy (1874–1925), *A Lady*

Moore, Lorrie (1957–), *What Is Seized*

Moses, Grandma (1860–1961)

Musset, Alfred de (1810–1857), *"Rappelle-toi"*

Nossis (3rd century B.C.), "Three Generations"

Oliphant, Margaret (1828–1897), *A Little Pilgrim*

Vera, Meshullam da (dates unknown), "Of Love and Lies"

Pliny the Younger (c. 61–c. 113), *Epistles*

Pope, Alexander (1688–1744), *An Essay on Man*, 1733–1734 (p. 92);
"Epitaph on Mrs. Corbet"(p. 85)

Púshkin, Aleksándr (1799–1837), "Grapes"

Riley, James Whitcomb (1849–1916), "Out to Old Aunt Mary's"

Rimbaud, Arthur (1854–1891), *"Oraison du soir"* (p. 8)

Rudagi (10th century), "Dyeing My Hair"

Schiller, Friedrich von (1759–1805), "Song of the Bell"

Shakespeare, William (1564–1616), *As You Like It*, 1598–1600 (p. 103);
King Richard III, 1592–1593 (p. 77)

Sigourney, Lydia Howard (1791–1865), "Establishment of a Female
College in New-Grenada, South America"

Songs of Milarepa (11th century), "Milarepa's Meeting with Kar Chon
Repa"

Sophocles (c. 495–406 B.C.), *Oedipus at Kolonos*

Sullivan, Anne (1866–1939)

Thatcher, Margaret (1925–), *The Times*, March
4, 1989

Tsui, Kitty (20th century)

Virgil (70–19 B.C.), *Eclogues,* 37 B.C.

Vyázemsky, Prince Pëtr (1792–1878), "Evening"

Walker, Alice (1944–)

Wharton, Edith (1862–1937)

Whitlam, Mrs. Margaret (dates unknown)

Whitman, Walt (1819–1892), "The Sleepers"(p. 65)

Wilde, Oscar (1854–1900)

Williams, Terry Tempest (1955–), *Pieces of White Shell,* 1984

Wordsworth, William (1770–1850), "Ode: Intimations of Immortality,"
  1807

Thanks to Susanne Braham, Eve Leder,

Jodi Burger, Christina Newhard, Jane Mattes,

and Diana Hoffman for photos of

their beautiful grandmothers.

This book was set in Aqualine and Centaur.